waiting for hope
A STUDY ON THE BOOK OF MALACHI

MIRANDA EWING

Study Suggestions

We believe that the Bible is true, trustworthy, and timeless and that it is vitally important for all believers. These study suggestions are intended to help you more effectively study Scripture as you seek to know and love God through His Word.

SUGGESTED STUDY TOOLS

- A Bible

- A double-spaced, printed copy of the Scripture passages that this study covers. You can use a website like *www.biblegateway.com* to copy the text of a passage and print out a double-spaced copy to be able to mark on easily

- A journal to write notes or prayers

- Pens, colored pencils, and highlighters

- A dictionary to look up unfamiliar words

HOW TO USE THIS STUDY

Begin your study time in prayer. Ask God to reveal Himself to you, to help you understand what you are reading, and to transform you with His Word (Psalm 119:18).

Before you read what is written in each day of the study itself, read the assigned passages of Scripture for that day. Use your double-spaced copy to circle, underline, highlight, draw arrows, and mark in any way you would like to help you dig deeper as you work through a passage.

Read the daily written content provided for the current study day.

Answer the questions that appear at the end of each study day.

HOW TO STUDY THE BIBLE

The inductive method provides tools for deeper and more intentional Bible study. To study the Bible inductively, work through the steps below after reading background information on the book.

1 OBSERVATION & COMPREHENSION
Key question: What does the text say?

After reading the daily Scripture in its entirety at least once, begin working with smaller portions of the Scripture. Read a passage of Scripture repetitively, and then mark the following items in the text:

- Key or repeated words and ideas
- Key themes
- Transition words (Ex: therefore, but, because, if/then, likewise, etc.)
- Lists
- Comparisons and contrasts
- Commands
- Unfamiliar words (look these up in a dictionary)
- Questions you have about the text

2 INTERPRETATION
Key question: What does the text mean?

Once you have annotated the text, work through the following steps to help you interpret its meaning:

- Read the passage in other versions for a better understanding of the text.
- Read cross-references to help interpret Scripture with Scripture.
- Paraphrase or summarize the passage to check for understanding.
- Identify how the text reflects the metanarrative of Scripture, which is the story of creation, fall, redemption, and restoration.
- Read trustworthy commentaries if you need further insight into the meaning of the passage.

3 APPLICATION
Key Question: How should the truth of this passage change me?

Bible study is not merely an intellectual pursuit. The truths about God, ourselves, and the gospel that we discover in Scripture should produce transformation in our hearts and lives. Answer the following questions as you consider what you have learned in your study:

- What attributes of God's character are revealed in the passage?

    Consider places where the text directly states the character of God, as well as how His character is revealed through His words and actions.

- What do I learn about myself in light of who God is?

    Consider how you fall short of God's character, how the text reveals your sin nature, and what it says about your new identity in Christ.

- How should this truth change me?

    A passage of Scripture may contain direct commands telling us what to do or warnings about sins to avoid in order to help us grow in holiness. Other times our application flows out of seeing ourselves in light of God's character. As we pray and reflect on how God is calling us to change in light of His Word, we should be asking questions like, "How should I pray for God to change my heart?" and "What practical steps can I take toward cultivating habits of holiness?"

THE ATTRIBUTES OF GOD

ETERNAL

God has no beginning and no end. He always was, always is, and always will be.

HAB. 1:12 / REV. 1:8 / IS. 41:4

FAITHFUL

God is incapable of anything but fidelity. He is loyally devoted to His plan and purpose.

2 TIM. 2:13 / DEUT. 7:9
HEB. 10:23

GOOD

God is pure; there is no defilement in Him. He is unable to sin, and all He does is good.

GEN. 1:31 / PS. 34:8 / PS. 107:1

GRACIOUS

God is kind, giving us gifts and benefits we do not deserve.

2 KINGS 13:23 / PS. 145:8
IS. 30:18

HOLY

God is undefiled and unable to be in the presence of defilement. He is sacred and set-apart.

REV. 4:8 / LEV. 19:2 / HAB. 1:13

INCOMPREHENSIBLE & TRANSCENDENT

God is high above and beyond human understanding. He is unable to be fully known.

PS. 145:3 / IS. 55:8-9
ROM. 11:33-36

IMMUTABLE

God does not change. He is the same yesterday, today, and tomorrow.

1 SAM. 15:29 / ROM. 11:29
JAMES 1:17

INFINITE

God is limitless. He exhibits all of His attributes perfectly and boundlessly.

ROM. 11:33-36 / IS. 40:28
PS. 147:5

JEALOUS

God is desirous of receiving the praise and affection He rightly deserves.

EX. 20:5 / DEUT. 4:23-24
JOSH. 24:19

JUST

God governs in perfect justice. He acts in accordance with justice. In Him, there is no wrongdoing or dishonesty.

IS. 61:8 / DEUT. 32:4 / PS. 146:7-9

LOVING

God is eternally, enduringly, steadfastly loving and affectionate. He does not forsake or betray His covenant love.

JN. 3:16 / EPH. 2:4-5 / 1 JN. 4:16

MERCIFUL
God is compassionate, withholding from us the wrath that we deserve.

TITUS 3:5 / PS. 25:10
LAM. 3:22-23

OMNIPOTENT
God is all-powerful; His strength is unlimited.

MAT. 19:26 / JOB 42:1-2
JER. 32:27

OMNIPRESENT
God is everywhere; His presence is near and permeating.

PROV. 15:3 / PS. 139:7-10
JER. 23:23-24

OMNISCIENT
God is all-knowing; there is nothing unknown to Him.

PS. 147:4 / I JN. 3:20
HEB. 4:13

PATIENT
God is long-suffering and enduring. He gives ample opportunity for people to turn toward Him.

ROM. 2:4 / 2 PET. 3:9 / PS. 86:15

SELF-EXISTENT
God was not created but exists by His power alone.

PS. 90:1-2 / JN. 1:4 / JN. 5:26

SELF-SUFFICIENT
God has no needs and depends on nothing, but everything depends on God.

IS. 40:28-31 / ACTS 17:24-25
PHIL. 4:19

SOVEREIGN
God governs over all things; He is in complete control.

COL. 1:17 / PS. 24:1-2
1 CHRON. 29:11-12

TRUTHFUL
God is our measurement of what is fact. By Him we are able to discern true and false.

JN. 3:33 / ROM. 1:25 / JN. 14:6

WISE
God is infinitely knowledgeable and is judicious with His knowledge.

IS. 46:9-10 / IS. 55:9 / PROV. 3:19

WRATHFUL
God stands in opposition to all that is evil. He enacts judgment according to His holiness, righteousness, and justice.

PS. 69:24 / JN. 3:36 / ROM. 1:18

TIMELINE OF SCRIPTURE

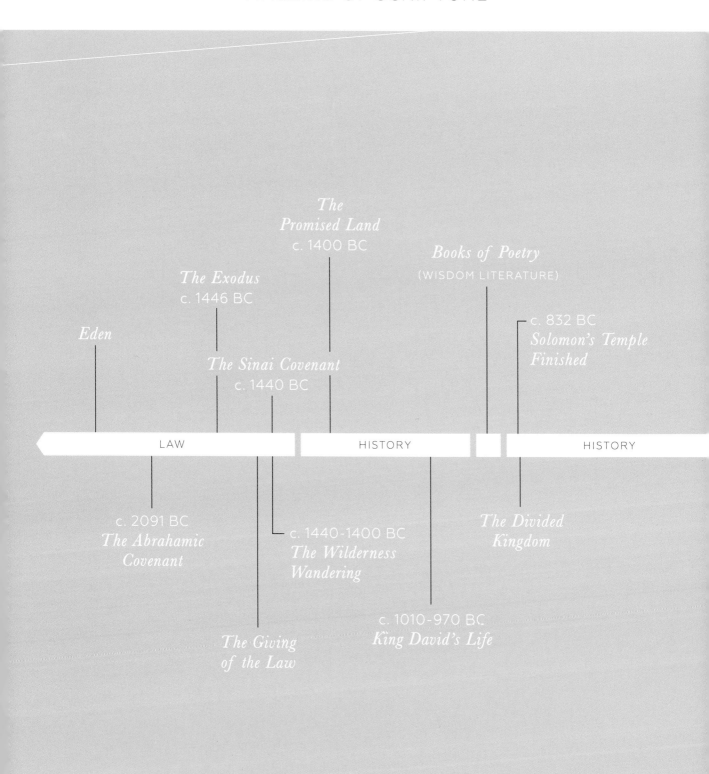

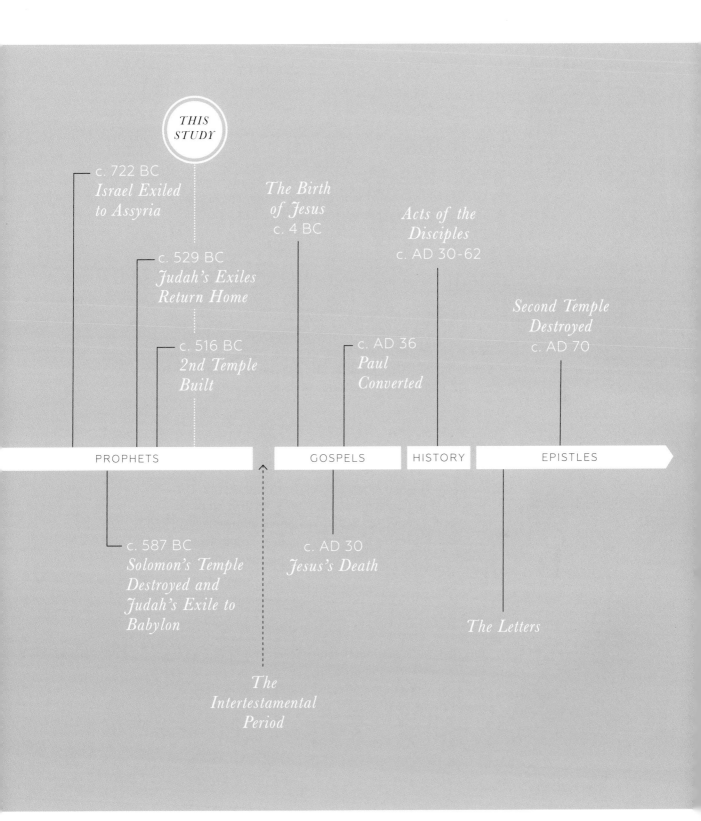

METANARRATIVE OF SCRIPTURE

Creation

In the beginning, God created the universe. He made the world and everything in it. He created humans in His own image to be His representatives on the earth.

Fall

The first humans, Adam and Eve, disobeyed God by eating from the fruit of the Tree of Knowledge of Good and Evil. Their disobedience impacted the whole world. The punishment for sin is death, and because of Adam's original sin, all humans are sinful and condemned to death.

Redemption

God sent His Son to become a human and redeem His people. Jesus Christ lived a sinless life but died on the cross to pay the penalty for sin. He resurrected from the dead and ascended into heaven. All who put their faith in Jesus are saved from death and freely receive the gift of eternal life.

Restoration

One day, Jesus Christ will return again and restore all that sin destroyed. He will usher in a new heaven and new earth where all who trust in Him will live eternally with glorified bodies in the presence of God.

"In this short book that closes the Old Testament, the Messiah is promised again."

IN THIS STUDY

WEEK 1

Introduction to Malachi — 15
Background to Malachi — 19
Undeserved Covenant Love — 23
Meaningless Worship — 27
His Name Will Be Great Among the Nations — 31
Scripture Memory — 35
Weekly Reflection — 36

WEEK 2

Blessings and Curses	39
Sacred Relationships	43
The Coming of the Messenger	47
The Lord's Provision	51
The Righteous and the Wicked	55
Scripture Memory	59
Weekly Reflection	60

WEEK 3

The Day of the Lord	63
Living in Light of the End	67
Remember His Word	71
After the Old Testament	75
The Gospel in Malachi	81
Scripture Memory	85
Weekly Reflection	86

"Covenant love means God has promised to love His people forever, regardless of how they love Him."

WEEK 1

INTRODUCTION TO MALACHI

The book of Malachi is the last book of the Old Testament, and it is also the last work of the minor prophets. It is only four chapters made up of fifty-five verses. Nonetheless, it contains a profound message of continued covenant love between the Lord and His people, though they disregard and do not properly worship Him. Covenant love means God has promised to love His people forever, regardless of how they love Him. The book contains God's final words to His people before He is silent for 400 years. Just like the people await the day when God speaks, we await the day of Christ's return. We read the book of Malachi in anticipation of the end of God's great story.

The book calls the people of Israel to return to the Law of the Lord and eagerly anticipate the coming of a "messenger." The promise of this messenger will first find fulfillment in John the Baptist and then will ultimately be fulfilled in Jesus Christ. The book of Malachi also highlights various themes, including the importance of priests who honor God, God's use of blessings and curses throughout the Old Testament, and the sacredness of marriage. However, the overall message of the book of Malachi reveals how the world will someday be a sanctified Zion where all people who love the Lord will rejoice and worship Him. "Zion" is another name for Jerusalem, the city of God, and it is used throughout Scripture to refer to heaven. Malachi is one last word of eternal hope in the Old Testament.

The only thing we know about the author of this book is his name: Malachi. "Malachi" means "my messenger." From studying the book of Nehemiah, we know that Malachi was probably one of his contemporaries, based on the similarity between their messages to the people of Israel. The events of Malachi generally took place in the post-exilic era, which took place after the Israelites returned home from their exile in Babylon. Babylon had fallen to the Persian empire, and King Cyrus of Persia gave a decree to allow the people of Israel to return to their homeland in 538 BC. Yet, they were still under his authority. Most scholars place Malachi as being written about 100 years after Cyrus's decree, between 450 and 430 BC.

It is helpful to do a brief review of Old Testament history up to this point to situate the book in its historical context. As such, the following paragraphs contain a brief history of the Old Testament as Malachi is the last book we read before the New Testament opens.

History began with the creation of the universe and humanity in Genesis. God's creation was good, but Adam's sin in the first few chapters of Genesis resulted in the fall of man and the curse of death. From that time, sin spread like an infectious disease so that the fullness of man's heart and intentions were completely evil. As God pronounced the curse of sin in the garden, He promised a Redeemer who would restore God's people and creation. Many years later, He made a covenant with a man named Abraham, promising that the Messiah would come through his offspring and be a blessing to the world. And while Abraham and his family lived a nomadic lifestyle, God promised Abraham that He would bring him and his family to the land He had given them. God's promise to make Abraham a great nation began to find its fulfillment in the Israelites, Abraham's descendants. The Israelites multiplied to incredible numbers and became slaves in Egypt. God used a man named Moses to deliver them from slavery and lead them through the wilderness. There, God made a covenant with them, a sacred promise between Himself and the people, through the giving of the Law.

Despite the Israelites' frequent stumbling, God delivered them into the land He promised Abraham. The people were then led by judges and kings, all proving themselves to be insufficient to rule God's people in righteousness, but God promised that a better king would come. God made a covenant with one of their kings, David, and promised that David's offspring would rule righteously over God's people on an eternal throne. The wickedness of the human kings who ruled over Israel after David led to the kingdom dividing into the Northern Kingdom, known as Israel, and the Southern Kingdom, called Judah, in 930 BC. Judah remained under the rule of Davidic kings.

Eventually, the wickedness and rebellion of both kingdoms would lead to their exile from the Promised Land in 722 BC and 586 BC. Israel would be conquered by the Assyrians first, and then Judah would be led into captivity by the Babylonians. The narrative of the Old Testament that follows these events focuses primarily on the captives of Judah in Babylon.

The Babylonian Empire was very powerful, but they were eventually defeated by Cyrus, King of Persia. The Israelite captives in Babylon were then taken into the Persian Empire. God would use Cyrus to send His people back to the Promised Land, where they would rebuild the city of Jerusalem, its wall, and the temple. They would even re-establish the priesthood, the men of Israel who helped God's people atone for their sin. The temple was not as glorious as the days of David, but the people continued to wait for the Messiah who had been foretold by the prophets. The people did not know it yet, but this Messiah would be the Redeemer who would restore creation. This King from the line of David was the One who would make all things right.

The book of Malachi is addressed to the Israelites who are waiting. They are one nation again, no longer split into two kingdoms. However, things are not as they once were. King Solomon's temple has been destroyed, and the new temple they have rebuilt is not as glorious as the original. The people are not their own independent nation and still live in the Persian empire. All of the earlier prophets' promises of a future hope and deliverance by the long-awaited Messiah seem to have fallen flat. They would continue to wait for many years after the message of Malachi was given. But in this short book that closes the Old Testament, the Messiah is promised again. God assures His people that the Day of the Lord is coming and that for those who faithfully follow Him, this day will be one of great healing and joy.

HOW DOES THE CONTEXT OF MALACHI IN THE STORY OF SCRIPTURE HELP YOU TO UNDERSTAND ITS MESSAGE?

HOW DOES KNOWING THE HISTORICAL BACKGROUND OF THE BOOK OF MALACHI HELP YOU UNDERSTAND THIS PROPHETIC BOOK'S PURPOSE?

WHAT DO YOU THINK WE MIGHT GAIN FROM THE MESSAGE OF MALACHI TODAY?

"The book of Malachi is addressed to the Israelites who are waiting."

WEEK 1

BACKGROUND TO MALACHI

Before you begin studying the entire book of Malachi passage by passage, take some time to read through the book in its entirety. It might be helpful to print out a copy of the text since it is such a short book. Make sure there is lots of space for notes on your copy to mark repeated ideas, phrases, and words. Also, take brief notes on your copy of the text about what you learn of the Lord's character, any parts of the passages that point you to the gospel, and some of your first takeaways. Use the provided questions in this section to summarize what you learned. You can return to this section at the end of the study to see how your understanding grows.

questions before you begin

WHAT KEY THEMES, WORDS, OR CONCEPTS DID YOU NOTICE IN THE BOOK OF MALACHI?

WHAT WAS ONE VERSE THAT STUCK OUT TO YOU THE MOST AS YOU READ? WHY?

WHAT DID YOU OBSERVE ABOUT THE CHARACTER OF GOD IN
THE BOOK OF MALACHI?

WHAT QUESTIONS DO YOU HAVE AFTER READING THROUGH THE ENTIRE BOOK?

WRITE A PRAYER ASKING GOD TO REVEAL MORE OF HIMSELF TO YOU
THROUGH THIS STUDY.

"God mercifully saved us because He first loved us."

WEEK 1

UNDESERVED COVENANT LOVE

READ MALACHI 1:1-6, GENESIS 25:27-26:6

Do you believe that the Lord truly loves you? In Ephesians 3:17-19, Paul prays that the church in Ephesus would be able to comprehend the depths of the Lord's love since they are rooted and established in it. The Lord's love defines everything about us when we belong to Him, but since we live in a world that has rejected God and are prone to turn back to sin, we often forget His love. We may even question it because of our circumstances. The Lord's people did the same when Malachi delivered his message.

Throughout the book, the prophet Malachi will present six disputes between the Lord and His people. The structure of the disputes is a repeated pattern. The Lord says something to Israel about how they have dishonored Him. The people then question Him or argue with what He says. Finally, the Lord affirms what He has said previously and expands the charge He brings against them. Malachi 1:1-6 contains the first dispute, but it falls slightly out of pattern with the structure mentioned above.

The first few words the Lord speaks to the people of Israel are strikingly beautiful: "I have loved you." It is important to pause here and note that though the Lord is about to state several ways the people have sinned against Him, He first reminds them of His steadfast, covenant love for them. To say that God has covenant love for Israel means He has promised to love them forever. And as the Lord speaks these first words to His people, He instantly declares that He has kept His covenant to them, though they have been faithless. "I have loved you" has been the cry of the Lord to His people from generation to generation, even as they continue to reject Him, fail to be faithful in their covenant relationship to Him, and turn to the gods of other nations. The Lord loves them regardless.

Israel's response to the Lord sarcastically questions Him: "How have you loved us?" To Israel, the situation they find themselves in seems to evidence God's abandonment rather than His love. They are still under the rule of a foreign nation, many of their exiled people have not returned home, their temple is only a shadow of what it once was, and the Messiah, the promised descendant of Abraham and David who will deliver Israel, has still not come. Things are not like the glorious days of old when King David and his son, Solomon, reigned.

God responds to their question by telling them He has loved Jacob and hated Esau. This may seem confusing at first, and we must go back to Old Testament history to understand what the Lord is saying. A man named Abram and his wife, Sarai, had once been pagans in the land of Ur before the Lord called them to follow Him. They followed His call, and the Lord made a covenant with them. He even changed their names. Abram became "Abraham," and Sarai became "Sarah." The Lord also told Abraham that he would have many descendants, even though he and his wife were old and barren. Through Abraham's offspring, all the nations of the earth would be blessed. The blessing and covenant God made with Abraham were passed down to his son, Isaac.

Isaac and his wife, Rebekah, had twin boys named Esau and Jacob. Esau was born before Jacob, so he was technically the firstborn son, though they were twins. By human accounts and cultural standards, we would assume that the blessing of the Lord would belong to Esau, but the Lord told their mother before they were born, "the older will serve the younger" (Genesis 25:23). Later in the story of the twin boys, this promise comes to fruition. Esau sells his birthright to his younger brother Jacob for a bowl of stew because he is so famished from hunting. By selling his birthright to Jacob, Esau gave away his position as spiritual leader of their family and the inherited covenant that God made with Abraham. God promised land, a nation full of descendants, and a Messiah through the covenant. Jacob deceitfully used his brother's hunger to his advantage, but Esau was willing to trade something precious to merely satisfy a temporary physical need. The Lord would rename Jacob "Israel," and this would be the name by which the covenant people of God would be known.

Esau's descendants, the Edomites, lived in direct opposition to the ways of the Lord. They sometimes even fought against Israel and helped the nation's other enemies come against them. And while the world may have seen the Edomites as blessed because of their immense wealth, possession of earthly treasure does not determine whether God favors a person. Although Esau's descendants were wealthy, the Lord rejected them. Eventually, the Lord made the Edomites' land a "wasteland," and He gave their inheritance to the "desert jackals" (Malachi 1:3). He also promised Israel that He would stop any attempt of the Edomites to recover from His destruction of them. His covenant was not with them (Malachi 1:4).

However, we must not make the mistake of thinking that the Lord made His covenant with Israel because they possessed righteousness the Edomites did not have. On the contrary, Israel constantly rebelled against the Lord through all of the Old Testament. Even Jacob, the brother of Esau, was known for his disobedience to God. The Lord's covenant love was because of His own faithfulness, mercy, and grace.

In the same way, God has chosen to save us. We were once dead in sin, but God mercifully saved us because He first loved us. And just as He showed His covenant love to Israel by defeating their enemies, God showed His covenant love to us by sending His Son, Jesus, to die for the penalty of our sins, defeating our enemies of sin and death forever. We do not deserve His love, but He graciously gives Himself to us. And because of this we, like Israel, can testify to the Lord's greatness—His greatness went beyond the borders of Israel to all of the nations with the hope of the gospel in Jesus Christ, and that greatness is daily displayed to us through His loving-kindness. He is ours forever, and we are His.

HOW DOES THE LORD'S PRONOUNCEMENT OF LOVE FOR ISRAEL, DESPITE
THEIR REJECTION OF HIM, REMIND YOU OF HOW THE LORD HAS LOVED YOU?
HOW IS THIS ENCOURAGING?

———

WHY WAS ESAU'S REJECTION OF HIS BIRTHRIGHT SUCH A SERIOUS SIN?
HOW MIGHT PEOPLE COMMIT A SIMILAR SIN TODAY?

———

WHY CAN LOOKING AT YOUR CIRCUMSTANCES AS THE EVIDENCE
OF GOD'S LOVE FOR YOU BE HARMFUL AND OUT OF LINE WITH WHAT
GOD SAYS IN HIS WORD?

———

"We have a great King who is worthy of our worship."

WEEK 1   *day four*

MEANINGLESS WORSHIP

READ MALACHI 1:6-10, DEUTERONOMY 32:3-14

As the Lord begins His second dispute with His covenant people, He turns His attention to their worship. The Lord was greatly displeased with the people's lack of devotion to Him. As we read this passage, it is wise to consider how we might have a low view of God like the Israelites and how this view may affect our worship of the Lord.

Worship goes beyond singing to the Lord during church. Worship is the honor and reverence we show to God through our lives. Worship is pouring out our lives to glorify the Lord. And if we are honest, our lives often display more worship for ourselves or other people and things than for God. In this passage in Malachi, while the Lord is addressing the worship of the people, He specifically reprimands the priests' actions.

The Lord is gracious again with His people by reminding them of who He is. He is their Father and Master. As Father, God is Israel's Creator who chose her for His own possession and has lovingly looked after her. He is also Israel's Redeemer. He saved them from slavery in Egypt, provided for them in the wilderness, helped them find a home in the Promised Land, was with them as they were taken captive by foreign enemies and exiled, and then enabled them to return home. He has upheld His covenant to the people of Israel, but they have not honored and obeyed their Father who loves them (Deuteronomy 10:12-13).

The priests, in particular, have "despised" His name (Malachi 1:6). To despise Him meant that they had an attitude of continual disrespect. They considered worshiping Him a worthless and irrelevant act. While the priests probably never vocalized these sentiments aloud, it was evident in how they carried out their sacrificial duties. They were accepting blind, lame, and sick animals for sacrifices. Under Levitical law, these animals should never have been brought to the altar of the Lord (Leviticus 22:22).

The Lord challenges the priests by telling them they would never bring unacceptable sacrifices to their governor. The priests and people would most likely bring their best animals and food from their homes to offer as a gift to this man.

It would be unthinkable to bring a lame or sick animal, and he would not accept it. So then, why would the Lord, the great King and their loving Father, accept these unacceptable sacrifices? He deserved their wholehearted devotion.

The temple was God's dwelling place with man. The temple existed to show Israel that their heavenly Father wanted to be with them and that by offering sacrifices, He would remove the penalty of their sins from them. The offered sacrifices brought them from an unclean to a holy state. The priests despised what allowed them to be with God, and by doing so, they despised God Himself. And while this grievance is true of all of Israel, the priests were the spiritual leaders among the people. If they did not revere God, the people would not care for Him either.

After disregarding the altar of the Lord, the priests and the people then asked Him for favors! They wanted Him to be gracious to them. The Lord does not base His grace and love for His people on their actions. He will always be faithful, but it was callous of them to treat Him so disrespectfully and then expect Him to act on their behalf. They wanted Him in their lives only when it was convenient to them.

What the Lord says next is heartbreaking. He says He would prefer them to close the temple doors and not offer any sacrifices to Him. This might perhaps give the Israelites the same feeling we would have if our churches were forced to close indefinitely, with no online gathering option. The temple and the sacrificial system were at the center of Israelite culture. To not have temple access would likely cause them to question their identity.

The Lord is grieved over the lack of love and devotion His people have toward Him. He does not need their sacrifices. He is completely self-sufficient. He chooses to dwell with His people in the temple and allows them to offer sacrifices so they can be with Him, but they do not understand who He is and that He belongs to them. All they can see is their loss and how things are not what they once were—that there seems to be no hope of things returning to what was. Their bitterness and hopelessness have squelched their love for God.

In all of this heaviness, the hope of Christ is magnified. Jesus is the Great High Priest who intercedes for the sins of His people by offering Himself as the last and final sacrifice. Every year, the high priest of Israel would enter the presence of God by going behind the curtain that separated the ark of the covenant from the people (Leviticus 16). The ark was where God chose to dwell with Israel. It was His throne room in their midst. The high priest would come before the Lord to make atonement for the sins of the people on this day, and the high priest would also have to make atonement for his own sins because no priest was completely righteous. Though they were charged with leading the people to the Lord, they struggled themselves.

But Jesus will show His Father the honor and fear He deserves—the honor and fear the priests who came before Jesus could never perfectly display, even when they tried. He will eliminate the sacrificial system because He is the perfect sacrifice—the perfect Passover Lamb. The temple is no longer necessary because His life, death, and resurrection allow people to have fellowship with God. God now resides in man through the Holy Spirit. We have become a temple for the Most High. He dwells within us.

We, too, are like Israel and forget who God is and how much we need Him. Our worship and devotion suffer as a result. We often do not offer Him our best. We do not devote ourselves to Him and instead devote ourselves to our various hobbies and pastimes, and then we ask Him to act on our behalf. Why do we so often treat our gracious King with so little regard? We are prone to wander and forget, so we must remind ourselves day by day of the glories of the gospel and the riches of His grace. We have a great King who is worthy of our worship.

HOW IS CHRIST A GREATER AND BETTER PRIEST THAN THE ONES DESCRIBED IN THIS PASSAGE? READ HEBREWS 4:14-5:10 TO AID IN YOUR UNDERSTANDING.

―――――

IN WHAT WAYS HAVE YOU NOT OFFERED YOUR BEST TO GOD, AND HOW HAS THAT IMPACTED YOUR RELATIONSHIP WITH HIM AND OTHERS?

―――――

HOW COULD YOU GIVE GOD THE BEST OF YOUR TIME, ENERGY, AND DEVOTION?

―――――

"Jesus is the fulfillment of every future hope and promise."

WEEK 1

HIS NAME WILL BE GREAT AMONG THE NATIONS

READ MALACHI 1:11-14

While God chose the people of Israel to be His possession and to be separate from the surrounding nations, God's intention was for all nations to come to know Him. Throughout the story of Scripture, God uses the people of Israel as messengers to the world that there is one true God, and He is worthy of worship!

As Malachi continues his critique of Israel's priests, he reminds the priests and Israel of who God is. He is the Lord of Armies. He is a great King. And God's name will be great and feared among the nations, even as they treat Him with contempt. The priests dishonored God in their heartless worship and acceptance of unworthy sacrifices, but there is future glory coming in which the whole world will be won for God, and His name will be worshiped in every place!

The people of Israel were very focused on their present lives, and though they had many promises from the prophets of future blessing, hope, and restoration, they saw nothing but hardship and an absence of God's provision. But this simply was not true. Even though Israel's land and temple were not fully restored to their previous state, Israel had been saved from exile by the Lord! Under Persian rule, they were able to worship Him again and allowed to return to their homeland to rebuild a temple. But Israel and her priests wanted more, though they had all they needed. They had the Lord, the Great King, and the promise of a future hope, but they considered worshiping Him to be wearisome.

We are not above the priests and people of Israel. Our hope is so often placed in our present life, and we forget that Christ's kingdom is at hand. Even though we cannot visibly see it, we are a part of it. And someday, this invisible kingdom that joins believers across the world into one body and family will be visible. We will see our great King, and we will live in His presence and worship Him forever! Our worship today reveals our view of the Lord and our belief in our future hope. If we are apathetic about being with the Lord, reading our Bibles, seeking Him in prayer, or singing praises to Him, we likely need to pause and consider how we think about the Lord. We are prone to forgetfulness, just like the people of

Israel. And we are also prone to discontentment as they were, even though He has given us everything we need in Himself. The more we study His attributes and understand His character, the more we will love Him! He is the fulfillment of all our desires, longings, hopes, and dreams.

Even the priests, God's representatives to the people, had forgotten the majesty of God. They looked at their priestly duties with contempt and thought they were tedious. They allowed the people of Israel to offer animals that were stolen, lame, or sick, which the Lord forbade. This should cause us as well to pause and consider the sacrifices we bring before the Lord. Jesus is the Great High Priest who offered Himself as the final and perfect sacrifice, eliminating our need for the sacrificial system, yet we still bring sacrifices of devotion to the Lord. These are not for our salvation but simply because we love our King. Do we give Him our second best? How do our gifts of time, money, worship, and even our very selves and our plans reflect our view of God?

It is wise to reflect on these things regularly. There will be seasons when we do not feel like leaping for joy because of our relationship with God. We could feel burned out, apathetic, indifferent, or even angry toward God because of current situations we are facing. But our feelings cannot determine our worship and view of God.

As we seek to remember who God is and praise Him in awe of His goodness and perfect character, our awe turns to all Christ accomplished by coming to the world in the person of Jesus. Jesus's offering of Himself has allowed the whole world to worship Him, and someday, the whole world will worship Him when He returns (Philippians 2:10). He is the fulfillment of God's promise to bless all of the nations through the offspring of Abraham (Genesis 12:1-3). And He is the King from David's line who will rule forever (2 Samuel 7:12-16). Jesus is the fulfillment of every future hope and promise, and though the Israelites did not know who He was as they heard Malachi prophesy about God's name being made great among the nations, we do. How much more reverent should our worship be in light of this truth.

JESUS'S OFFERING OF HIMSELF HAS ALLOWED THE WHOLE WORLD to worship Him

HOW HAS THE LORD'S NAME BECOME GREAT THROUGHOUT THE NATIONS, JUST LIKE HE PROMISED?

———

WHY IS IT IMPORTANT TO MEDITATE ON THE LORD AND HIS PROVISION RATHER THAN THE THINGS WE BELIEVE WE LACK?

———

HOW HAVE YOU GIVEN GOD YOUR SECOND BEST? WHAT IS A PRACTICAL STEP YOU CAN TAKE TO CHANGE?

———

week one Scripture *memory*

MALACHI 1:11

"MY NAME WILL BE GREAT AMONG THE NATIONS,
FROM THE RISING OF THE SUN TO ITS SETTING.
INCENSE AND PURE OFFERINGS WILL BE PRESENTED
IN MY NAME IN EVERY PLACE BECAUSE MY NAME
WILL BE GREAT AMONG THE NATIONS,"
SAYS THE LORD OF ARMIES.

week one reflection

PARAPHRASE A SECTION FROM THIS WEEK'S PASSAGE THAT STOOD OUT TO YOU THE MOST.

WHAT DID YOU OBSERVE FROM THIS WEEK'S TEXT ABOUT GOD AND HIS CHARACTER?

WHAT DOES THIS PASSAGE TEACH YOU ABOUT THE CONDITION OF MANKIND AND YOURSELF?

REVIEW MALACHI 1:1-14

HOW DOES THIS PASSAGE POINT TO THE GOSPEL?

IN LIGHT OF WHAT YOU HAVE READ, HOW SHOULD YOU RESPOND TO THIS PASSAGE?

WHAT ARE TWO ACTION STEPS YOU CAN TAKE THIS WEEK TO APPLY THIS PASSAGE TO YOUR LIFE?

"God's blessing and discipline are always meant to lead us back to Him and grow us in Christlikeness."

WEEK 2 — *day one*

BLESSINGS AND CURSES

READ MALACHI 2:1-9, HEBREWS 12:1-11

In the previous verses of Malachi, the Lord addressed how the priests wronged Him and dishonored His name. He now will show them how their sin led to their need for correction. The decree we find in today's passage is for Israel and its spiritual leaders. But the verses we read today reveal one way He shows His love for His children—He disciplines us.

God begins by declaring His love to His people, but He quickly reveals how they had gone astray. All of His rebukes were evidence of the depths of His love because by correcting Israel, He was still giving them a chance to repent. But in verse 2 of chapter 2, the Lord warns the priests that if they do not listen to what He has said, they will face curses from His hand. These curses would even affect the blessings He gave them.

We may pause while reading these verses. *The Lord sends curses? That does not seem like something He would do.* But the language the Lord uses in this passage would have been very familiar to the Hebrew people. In Deuteronomy 28, Moses gave Israel a list of blessings that would occur if the people were faithful to follow God's commands, and he also gave them a list of curses that would result from disobedience. It seems as though the Lord needed to remind His people that some of the difficulties they were already facing were not just coincidences. They were curses from His hand, meant to draw them back to Him.

But why would God send curses to discipline His people? The answer has everything to do with who God is and who we are. God is completely holy, and He is at war with sin that has marred His creation. But in His great compassion, He had mercy on the people of Israel and covered them with His love. He was consistently faithful to them, even when they rejected Him and worshiped other gods. The Lord brought them back into fellowship with Himself, and He saved them from their enemies. Best of all, He promised that there would be a Messiah from their offspring—One who would save them and many other nations forever.

Everything God did was for their good because He is good. His love for them was perfect. There is nothing questionable about it. By placing curses on them, God was trying to call His people's attention to what was truly harming them—sin. He wants them to realize through experiencing these curses that they need Him; otherwise, they will surely perish. The curse is meant to bring them back to blessing.

Though the Lord is brokenhearted over the sin of the priests, He wants to be restored to them. He wants the covenant that He made with the tribe of Levi to continue (Malachi 2:4). And in order to show them what they are missing by continuing in disobedience, He reminds them of what this covenant had once been like.

The priests of Levi experienced a covenant of peace with God because they feared the Lord. They properly revered His name. This, in turn, caused them to speak the truth and act with integrity. Because of the former priests' reverence for God, they were able to turn many Israelites from sin.

Pause for a moment, and remember something from Israel's history—the first priest from the tribe of Levi, Aaron, was not a perfect man. He had a covenant of peace with God. But when he began, he actually helped lead the Israelites astray in their worship. When Moses climbed up to the top of Mount Sinai and was nowhere to be found for days, Levi caved under the pressure of the Israelites and helped them create a golden calf to worship (Exodus 32:1-6). He did not hesitate to answer their wicked request to make another god. Aaron fashioned the calf and built an altar before it. He called the calf by the name of the Lord and issued a proclamation that the people would have a feast dedicated to this idol.

How could this man be described as someone who spoke truth and walked in integrity? Aaron repented of his sin but faced tragic consequences. A total of 3,000 Israelites were put to death for idol worship, and a devastating plague was sent to the camp of Israel. All of this happened so that God could restore Aaron and His people to Himself. The sin of spiritual leaders has consequences for all who follow them, but God's heart is to restore His own.

The description of Levi in Malachi 2:5-7 is only perfectly fulfilled in our Great High Priest, Jesus Christ. Jesus became our High Priest when He went forward to atone for our sins on the cross. Through His sacrifice, He gives all of us a covenant of life and peace with God. His words are true, and His life was lived in complete integrity. He saves those from all sin who love Him. And He makes a way for broken leaders and people like Levi to be restored by faith and become new creations. He gives them His own integrity where they have fallen short.

This passage in Malachi shows us the critical role of spiritual leadership. It is easy for those who lead God's people to become spiritually lazy, but the consequences are severe. The sin of pastors and church leaders can wrongly become a reason for some to walk away from their faith. However, He will discipline these leaders and the people who follow them in order for His people to have life.

When restoration is achieved and the leaders of God's church are in a right relationship with Him, they can properly encourage and teach God's people what is true. Love and adoration for the Lord are renewed, and the world can see the glory of the good news of Christ.

God's blessing and discipline are always meant to lead us back to Him and grow us in Christlikeness. It is for our joy, though it may be painful. Discipline should not cause us to lose heart or grow weary, like the verses in Hebrews instruct. It should instead cause us to look to the Lord, remember we are His children, and know that everything He allows in our lives, He works for His glory and our good. We can trust Him as we wrestle against sin because He desires to give us His "peaceful fruit of righteousness" (Hebrews 12:11). God's discipline is one way He calls us His own.

IN LIGHT OF THE CRITICAL ROLE OUR SPIRITUAL LEADERS PLAY IN OUR LIVES AND THE LIVES OF OTHERS, WHAT ARE WAYS YOU CAN ENCOURAGE YOUR OWN LEADERS TOWARD THE LORD?

IN THIS PASSAGE OF MALACHI, THE LORD SHOWS US HOW THE SINS OF A SPIRITUAL LEADER CAN AFFECT MANY PEOPLE BESIDES HIMSELF. WHAT SINS IN YOUR LIFE AFFECT THE PEOPLE AROUND YOU? WHO MIGHT YOU NEED TO APOLOGIZE TO BECAUSE OF THIS? AND HOW MIGHT RESTORATION CHANGE YOUR RELATIONSHIP WITH THIS PERSON?

WHY SHOULD THE LORD'S DISCIPLINE IN YOUR OWN LIFE BRING YOU TO LOVE AND TRUST THE LORD?

"We can look to Christ, the bridegroom who was and is faithful to His bride."

WEEK 2

SACRED RELATIONSHIPS

READ MALACHI 2:10-16

The last few passages we have studied of Malachi have mostly been directed toward the spiritual leaders of Israel, and rightfully so. If the priests of the Lord dishonored His name, their actions and behavior would influence the people for whom they were responsible. But in today's verses, we see not only the priests acting wickedly before the Lord but all of Judah.

At the beginning of verse 10, the narration switches from the Lord back to the prophet Malachi. He questions Judah and wonders if they truly know who created them and understand that they all belonged to God. He was their Father. Yet, they had no right to worship Him. Malachi tells them that they have acted detestably toward God and each other. What they have done has profaned — treated with contempt or irreverence — the Lord's sanctuary (Malachi 2:11).

So what have they done? What is their heinous crime? The text says that the people have "married the daughter of a foreign god" (Malachi 2:11). This means that the men of Judah were intermarrying with women of other nations who worshiped different gods. In the same way that the men and women of Judah were children of the Lord, these women were the daughters of the gods they worshiped. And the men of Judah were bringing these women into the family of God, which meant that their false gods were also being introduced to God's people.

This is why Malachi tells the people they profane the Lord's temple by intermarrying with those who do not love the Lord. Judah was meant to be set apart for God, but they accepted the false gods of their foreign spouses. By bringing their foreign wives into Judah, they were also bringing false gods into God's sanctuary. When they did this, the men of Judah endangered the whole community of God. Little by little, acceptance for these false gods would grow and grow. This acceptance would bleed into many parts of the people's lives — most importantly, their own relationships with the one true God.

Their crime against the Lord was serious, and Malachi tells them that whoever participated in this sin would be cut off by the Lord. Perhaps some of the men who had intermarried were already beginning to experience this consequence.

The Lord was not answering their groans or cries to Him, even though they wept loudly and publicly covered His altar with their tears.

But the Lord would not listen because while the men of Judah were marrying foreign wives, they were also forsaking their own wives. They were divorcing the women they had married in their youth, and because of this, the Lord was further dishonored, and their wives were shamed. God had established a covenant between these men and their wives. He gave them a portion of His Spirit to unite them in marriage. Through the covenant of marriage, He called them to imitate the covenant relationship between Himself and the people of Israel. But when the men divorced their wives, they tore this marriage covenant apart. Their love for their wives became hate, and they did not behave like children of God.

As we observe the state of Judah's relationships, we need to realize that our love for the Lord influences the love we show others. We will only truly recognize the people around us as image-bearers of Christ when we know who God is and worship Him as Creator. When you love the Lord, you begin to love what and who He loves. Your heart grows for His family, the Church. And you desire His family to have unity and not disruption.

Problems in relationships can often be the source of disunity within God's people. Malachi gave the people of Judah two examples of this, and these situations still exist today. The disruption follows when believers marry unbelievers and when believers divorce. This is not to say that God cannot redeem a marriage in which one person is a believer and one person is not, nor is it to say that there is never a reason for divorce. However, Scripture is clear that severing the union of marriage, even if sometimes necessary, always leads to pain and brokenness.

The Lord wants His people to honor one another and to remember that followers of Christ are all united in Him. He is our Father. When we revere each other, we bring glory to the Lord. We stand out from a world that celebrates division. We participate in God's life-giving peace. We must watch ourselves carefully as the Lord instructs His people to do. We are all capable of harming one another in our own self-interest and desires.

But we can look to Christ, the bridegroom who was and is faithful to His bride. Jesus often spoke of Himself as a groom to help us understand the relationship between Himself and His people. There is great anticipation before a wedding between the groom and the bride, and in Jesus's culture and our culture today, the joy of a bride and groom uniting was and is worthy of celebration. Jesus is the perfect bridegroom. And unlike the grooms of Israel and today, Jesus makes His bride holy and righteous, and He will never leave her for another. Jesus will be true to the end. And one day, when the people of God are finally united with Him, we will feast and rejoice at His wedding celebration—the marriage supper of the Lamb (Revelation 19:9). We have so much to look forward to when we are finally reunited in Him, for we will never be separated from our faithful Groom, and He will free us from sin forever. The celebration will never end. This marriage supper will be just the beginning of forever in His presence.

WE WILL NEVER BE SEPARATED FROM OUR FAITHFUL GROOM.

HOW DOES CHRIST, THE FAITHFUL AND PERFECT BRIDEGROOM, GIVE US A MODEL TO FOLLOW FOR OUR MARRIAGES? HOW DOES HE OFFER REDEMPTION FOR MARRIAGES THAT HAVE BEEN BROKEN? SEE EPHESIANS 5:27-28.

GOD WAS SERIOUS ABOUT HIS PEOPLE NOT INTERMARRYING WITH THOSE WHO DID NOT LOVE HIM. HOW CAN ROMANTIC RELATIONSHIPS BETWEEN BELIEVERS AND NONBELIEVERS HURT THOSE INDIVIDUALS AND THE PEOPLE IN THEIR LIVES?

HOW HAVE YOU SEEN YOUR OWN LOVE FOR THE LORD AFFECT HOW YOU LOVE OTHERS?

"God is working in ways we do not know, and He will accomplish all that He has promised."

WEEK 2

THE COMING OF THE MESSENGER
READ MALACHI 2:17–3:5

Judah's dishonor of the Lord was widespread among the people. The priests scoffed at the Lord and offered Him half-hearted sacrifices. The people questioned the Lord's love for them and were breaking their marriage covenants. Things were falling apart, and God's people were acting more and more like the world.

We are not above their response to their situation. Malachi spoke to a group of people who remembered the days when their temple was glorious and their kings were renowned. But after Babylon destroyed Jerusalem and tore down Solomon's temple, the people's faith in God had been shaken. Even though He allowed them to return home, they still were not their own nation, and all the promises of a Messiah seemed to fall flat as they dealt with their Persian governors and king. They were tired—tired of waiting on God to do what He said He would and tired of seeing evil people win battles when, at one time, God delivered them from all of their enemies. They wondered if God was now rewarding evil, and thought maybe He was not a God of justice after all.

If we are honest with ourselves, we may often think some of the same things. We become tired of our evil-filled world, and sometimes it seems like the Lord lets evil prosper over good. We wonder where the Lord is and if He is coming soon. Our lack of faith in God is wearisome to Him. Just like the people of Judah, we can think poorly of His character, and so we must repent.

While Judah sat in discontentment and frustration with the Lord, they could not see what He was orchestrating. But Malachi gives them words from the Lord—a messenger is coming, one who will prepare the way for the Lord. The text says God will come to His temple, and He will bring the message of the covenant once again.

As we read these words, we wonder—who is this messenger? The answer to this is two-fold. All of the gospels point to Jesus's cousin, John the Baptist, as the messenger who prepared the way for the Lord. But these verses also describe the messenger as the Lord Himself since He is going to return to the temple and speak of His covenant to the people. While John the Baptist was the first messenger who prepared the people for the Messiah by preaching about the kingdom of God and baptizing those who repented and turned to God, the ultimate and final messenger is Jesus Christ.

This passage reveals the two different times Jesus would come as a messenger to earth. In His first coming, Jesus would proclaim the message of the gospel and redeem His people through His perfect life, sacrificial death on the cross on our behalf, and resurrection from the dead. He would be a messenger of God's covenant, but He would also establish a new covenant, one that the prophets spoke of before His arrival. Jesus would fulfill this covenant Himself on behalf of all who believe in Him because He will make peace between the Lord and those who love Him. His final offering for the sins of God's people would be pleasing to God. The sacrificial system would cease.

Jesus would refine the religious leaders of the day and even cleanse the temple during His ministry, but most of His refining work will come when He returns again. Jesus's second coming is when He will finally purge the world of sin, and death will be defeated forever. He will deliver the justice of God against all of the wicked. There will be no question how God views those who have disobeyed Him and rejected the gospel. Jesus's return will bring His answer.

The people to whom Malachi delivered the Lord's words had no idea that Jesus was coming, but when He did come, He came suddenly at a moment they did not expect. And so it will happen again. He is coming soon, just like He said. We do not know the day or hour, and "soon" does not necessarily mean quickly, though that might be our own definition. In the Lord's eyes, one day is as a thousand years (2 Peter 3:8). When He does come, the world will not anticipate His arrival, and it will not be able to escape His final judgment.

So as we wait on Him and anticipate the day we will be reunited with our beloved Savior, let us put our hope and trust in Christ. When we are frustrated with evil, let us hope in Him. When we long to be without pain and hardship, let us hope in Him. God is working in ways we do not know, and He will accomplish all that He has promised.

WHEN WE ARE FRUSTRATED WITH EVIL, LET US HOPE IN HIM. WHEN WE LONG TO BE WITHOUT PAIN AND HARDSHIP, *let us hope in Him.*

IN MALACHI 3:1, THE TEXT SUBTLY DISTINGUISHES BETWEEN THE TWO
MESSENGERS WHO ARE COMING. HOW DOES IT DO THIS, AND WHAT IS THE
DIFFERENCE BETWEEN THESE MESSENGERS?

―――――

HOW WAS JESUS A REFINER OF THE SONS OF LEVI IN HIS FIRST COMING?
HOW WILL HE REFINE THE WORLD IN HIS SECOND COMING?

―――――

HOW CAN WE REMEMBER ETERNITY, EVEN WHEN THE WORLD AROUND US
SEEMS TO GROW MORE EVIL AND DARK? HOW WILL REMEMBERING ETERNITY
CHANGE OUR PERSPECTIVE?

―――――

"God is the One we can trust."

WEEK 2

THE LORD'S PROVISION

READ MALACHI 3:6-12

Perhaps one of the best and most difficult things about being human is that we are prone to change. If we want to learn a new skill or quit a bad habit, it is within our ability. But our strong tendency toward change also hurts us. Even if we believe in Jesus and are following Him, it is easy for us to slide back into old habits. We are tempted by sin, and we struggle to follow Him consistently.

But the Lord is quite the opposite. He is unchanging. There is nothing He can learn because He already knows all things. He does not need to quit a bad habit, for all of His ways are perfect. He is steadfast and always the same. We can place our trust in Him. God, in His graciousness, has let the identity of His people be found in Himself and not in their inconsistency.

In verse 6 of chapter 3, the Lord powerfully tells His people that they are not consumed because He does not change. But another translation of this verse says that because the Lord does not change, they do not cease to be sons of Jacob (NEB). In other words, they do not cease to be His Sons. Jacob, the son of Isaac we discussed earlier in the study, was the patriarch whose name represented all of God's people. Jacob's name was changed to "Israel," and Israel would be the lasting name of Abraham's descendants. Thus, the people's identity was rooted in God.

The Lord tells them that they will never lose their status as God's sons and daughters because He never changes. As they sojourned through the world, they did not need to worry about this identity being taken from them. It was theirs forever. But instead of being reliant on God and resting in Him, they run from Him and disobey. His provision gave them everything they needed, but they became convinced that there was more to be had elsewhere.

Still, God calls His children to return, and He even gives them a plan for how to begin. He tells them not to rob Him by withholding their offerings. From these verses, we learn that the people are not only offering the Lord lame or blemished sacrifices but that some are not offering Him any at all.

Many people will use this passage to discuss only the amount we should give in an offering or tithe to God, but we cannot take it out of its context. The Lord did not need His people's contributions. He could accomplish what He needed to without them. But when the people robbed the Lord of a percentage of their harvest or earnings, they were really robbing themselves. God wanted His people to see Him as the source of their provision, and He wanted them to realize that when they worshiped and obeyed Him, they would be in fellowship with Him, which is their greatest blessing. By choosing to run from Him and try to provide for themselves, they were missing out on God's care and love for them. Because of this, the nations around them could not witness God's people living peacefully and bountifully from His generosity.

The people's forgetfulness of their identity led them to ignore God and what He asked them to do. God allowed their land to suffer as they experienced a curse from God. But God would quickly take this curse away if they would return to Him and trust Him. He longingly waited to bless His people and make them "a delightful land" (Malachi 3:12).

When we are forgetful of our identity in Christ and how our salvation has changed everything about who we are, we are prone to forget the beauty of the gospel. If we lose sight of our identity, we also will lose sight of our eternal home that is coming. We will live more for the troubles and worries of our day-to-day lives instead of viewing them in light of our inheritance in Christ. Most likely, we will not see the need to give back to the Lord.

Whatever your view is on how often and how much a believer should give, all believers can remain in agreement that we are to give back to the Lord from what He has provided. We believe the lie that everything we own was because of something we did, but really, it is all blessings from God's hand. We so easily twist these blessings and rely on them more than the One who provided them. God calls us to release our grip on our possessions, put them back into His hands, and watch Him work on our behalf. Our identity is found in Him, not in our material possessions or what we think we can do on our own. Our worldly possessions are passing away, and our self-sufficiency will fail us every time, but our identity in Christ is ours forever, for the Lord is unchanging and immovable. God is the One we can trust.

OUR WORLDLY POSSESSIONS ARE PASSING AWAY, AND OUR SELF-SUFFICIENCY WILL FAIL US EVERY TIME, BUT OUR IDENTITY IN CHRIST IS *ours forever.*

WHAT COMFORTS YOU IN KNOWING THAT THE LORD IS UNCHANGING?

HOW DO YOU ROB YOURSELF WHEN YOU REFUSE TO GIVE BACK TO THE LORD?

READ EPHESIANS 1-2. HOW DO OUR IDENTITY IN CHRIST AND ETERNAL INHERITANCE INFLUENCE HOW WE INTERACT WITH OUR MATERIAL POSSESSIONS?

"God has written our names in His book of remembrance."

WEEK 2

THE RIGHTEOUS AND THE WICKED

READ MALACHI 3:13-18

In today's verses, we read the last of God's oracles, or revelations, to the people. The subject of this revelation repeats a revelation that has already been given. The Lord once again addresses the people's belief that those who do evil are blessed, and those who walk in obedience to Him have nothing to gain for it. He describes "the day of the Lord" once more, but this time, God further explains what will happen to the righteous and the wicked on this day.

Because the people had forgotten their identity in Christ, they forgot their eternal inheritance. The Lord had promised them that they would one day be gathered to Him and live forever in the city of Zion, the place where God would physically be with man once more. Soon, there would be a Messiah who would deliver them from their enemies. But as they waited for God's promises, it seemed as if things were not really getting better. There seemed to be no deliverer to overthrow their foreign rulers. And though they had returned home from their exile in Babylon, things were not the same. The surrounding nations prospered while they wallowed away. Their glorious temple was gone. Many of their loved ones perished. So they questioned the Lord. They forgot His faithfulness and immediately began to wonder if following Him was worth it. They wanted deliverance and restoration now. They did not want to wait any longer.

The Lord tells them that their words are harsh against Him. In light of all that God had done for His people, they still chose to not believe what He promised them. They thought serving God was useless, and they believed those who are arrogant to be fortunate because they have tested God and not been punished. These are indeed bitter words against the Lord. They should cause us to pause and consider whether we think in similar ways at times. If we do, we need to come to the Lord in repentance. When the people heard this oracle from Malachi, it caused a group of those who believed in the Lord to pause and gather together.

While many people in Judah rejected God, there were some who had not. These people were God's faithful remnant. And as they came together, in repentance and sorrow over how their words and beliefs had grieved the Lord, the Lord immediately claimed ownership of them. Notice how He jumps to help them in verse 17. The Lord is delighted when we are quick to repent and turn our hearts to Him.

Malachi tells us that the Lord has a book of remembrance for the names of all of those who fear the Lord and highly regard His name. He shows the faithful that they will always be His, and even on the day when He returns to judge the world, they will not need to be afraid, for they will always belong to Him. He has compassion on them because they are His children. All of their longing for justice to be done will be satisfied as the Lord makes clear those who love Him and those who do not.

How difficult it is to go through life and see evil prosper. Though we have been waiting for the return of Christ for a long time, we must not believe the lie that God's promises are void and that it is useless to follow Him. God has written our names in His book of remembrance. We are His. On the day when He comes to bring final judgment and redeem the world, we will see all of His story completed. Sin and evil will be no more, and we will rejoice as Christ begins His reign in His physical kingdom.

When you are tempted to think and believe that God is not who He says, remember how He has been faithful. Dig into your Bible, and rehearse His promises to yourself. Know that how God brings about His plan for you may be different than what you planned, but He will be faithful to you nonetheless. If you have trusted Him as your Lord and Savior, you are His child, and your name is written in His book. He will never forsake you. He will show you compassion and mercy, and He will deliver you on the day when He comes again to judge the world and make all things right. Evil will not win, and His light will overcome the darkness.

Evil will not win, and His light will overcome the darkness.

WHY IS OUR CURRENT PHYSICAL OR SOCIAL CONDITION ON EARTH A POOR WAY OF TESTING WHETHER THE LORD KEEPS HIS PROMISES?

———

WHAT ENCOURAGEMENT DO YOU FIND IN KNOWING THAT THE LORD IS QUICK TO HELP THOSE WHO ARE REPENTANT?

———

WHAT ARE TWO PROMISES FROM SCRIPTURE ABOUT THE LORD YOU CAN REHEARSE TO YOURSELF WHEN YOU ARE TEMPTED TO BELIEVE HE IS NOT WHO HE SAYS HE IS? IF YOU ARE NEW TO READING THE BIBLE, WE RECOMMEND THAT YOU LOOK UP ROMANS 10:9, MATTHEW 11:28, MATTHEW 28:20B, ROMANS 8:38-39, AND LAMENTATIONS 3:22-23.

———

week two Scripture *memory*

MALACHI 3:6

BECAUSE I, THE LORD, HAVE NOT CHANGED, YOU DESCENDANTS OF JACOB HAVE NOT BEEN DESTROYED.

week two reflection

PARAPHRASE A SECTION FROM THIS WEEK'S PASSAGE THAT STOOD OUT TO YOU THE MOST.

WHAT DID YOU OBSERVE FROM THIS WEEK'S TEXT ABOUT GOD AND HIS CHARACTER?

WHAT DOES THIS PASSAGE TEACH YOU ABOUT THE CONDITION OF MANKIND AND YOURSELF?

REVIEW MALACHI 2:1-3:18

HOW DOES THIS PASSAGE POINT TO THE GOSPEL?

IN LIGHT OF WHAT YOU HAVE READ, HOW SHOULD YOU RESPOND TO THIS PASSAGE?

WHAT ARE TWO ACTION STEPS YOU CAN TAKE THIS WEEK TO APPLY THIS PASSAGE TO YOUR LIFE?

"Jesus is returning soon, and your response to who He is determines your experience on the day of the Lord."

WEEK 3 — *day one*

THE DAY OF THE LORD

READ MALACHI 4:1-3

The day of the Lord is an event mentioned many times throughout the Old Testament. Whenever it appears, it is often automatically associated with judgment and wrath. But for the believer, it is a day of great hope and joy, for it is a day when all of God's promises will be fulfilled, and we will be in His presence forever.

The book of Malachi tells us that God's people believed He did not fulfill His promises. They saw the wicked prosper and the righteous suffer, and they wondered how God could be just. But God declares at the end of this book that the day is coming when justice will be delivered. There will be no question over who is righteous and who is wicked. It will be made clear.

And so, as the book closes, God gives a description of this final day. The first detail He provides at the beginning of chapter 4 is that "the day is coming." The date is set for the Lord's arrival, and the time draws nearer and nearer. And this is not a day that will come quietly. The day of the Lord will come, "burning like a furnace" (Malachi 4:1). But why is it burning? When Jesus died on the cross, the wrath of God was poured onto Him for the people of God, but there is still wrath reserved for those who reject God and live in opposition to Him. God's wrath is for all sin, but the righteous blood of Christ has covered the believer's sin.

God's wrath for the sin and evil that plagues the world is still burning. And just like fire devours anything in its path, God's wrath will devour everything that is a perversion to His creation. He will not let it be tainted any longer. He will obliterate the curse of sin once and for all. When the day of the Lord reaches its end, the wicked will be gone. The passage says the Lord will reduce them to stubble, and they will be consumed.

These are difficult words to hear, and they are even more difficult if we have made a habit of only familiarizing ourselves with "happier" character traits of the Lord. However, His wrath works in tandem with His lovingkindness, and it is an attribute we should not ignore. God's wrath over evil shows the depths of His love. He will not let the wicked continue to hurt His people, and He will bring those who love Him safely into His presence. Even the fact that we can read and learn about the day of the Lord is evidence of His mercy. He has provided warning after warning of what is to come. When the people of the Lord initially heard this message from Malachi, Jesus had not yet arrived on earth. Before the world would face judgment, it would receive its Savior. This was yet another act of mercy from God.

But the day of the Lord will not be an unwelcome day for all people. For those who belong to God, the burning of this day will not feel like a devouring fire but rather like the warmth of a rising sun. It will bring healing and restoration to those who have believed in Christ, and it will cause all believers to go out and playfully leap like calves leaving their stalls. We will be free. We will rejoice in being released forever from the presence of sin, which no longer plagues us, and we will finally be able to love the Lord and others perfectly. We will be enthralled and overcome with joy at the Lord's arrival, the day for which we expectantly wait. The wicked will be no more. The Lord will win.

The Lord even says that His people will trample the wicked. God will invite us to participate in His judgment, and however we may feel about that presently, we will not hesitate to do so when He calls. We can trust Him with the details of that day, and we can trust Him as we wait now for its arrival. The Lord of Armies is coming, and He cannot be stopped. We serve a God who has all authority and power, and the day of the Lord will be an incredible demonstration of His love for His people and His victory over evil. The sin that has mangled and twisted God's creation will finally be destroyed, and we will get to be a part of its demise.

Do not forget that this day is coming. Let its severity motivate you to live, not for your earthly life that quickly passes away but for your life in heaven that is eternity with Christ. Remember the people God has placed in your life who do not believe and desperately need to hear the gospel. If they do not know Him, they will miss the healing and joy that the day of the Lord will bring, and the wrath of God will consume them. We must follow Christ's commission and tell the world that the righteous blood of Jesus can cover their sins, just as it has covered ours. May we not be apathetic toward those who are lost, for we too were once headed for destruction. Praise God for His mercy and the saving work of Christ on behalf of all who believe.

If you are not among God's people because you have never trusted in Christ as Savior, see this moment as a God-given opportunity to come to Him and be saved. Each one of us has been born into spiritual death because of the sins of Adam and Eve, the first man and woman God created. But God made a way for us to escape this death and have life through His Son, Jesus Christ. Jesus lived a perfect life and died on a cross for the sins of all who would come to know Him. But Jesus did not remain in the grave. He was raised to life three days later, and because of this, we also are able to be raised from spiritual death to life. All that God requires is for us to believe in Christ and confess Him as Lord. Jesus is returning soon, and your response to who He is determines your experience on the day of the Lord. Do not miss His healing righteousness and the glories of His grace. God offers forgiveness and eternal life to you at this very moment.

GOD OFFERS FORGIVENESS AND ETERNAL LIFE TO YOU AT THIS VERY MOMENT.

WHY IS IT IMPORTANT THAT WE ACKNOWLEDGE BOTH GOD'S LOVE AND HIS WRATH?

WHY IS KNOWING AND STUDYING THE CHARACTER OF GOD VITAL TO OUR SPIRITUAL GROWTH AND WELLBEING?

HOW DOES HEARING ABOUT THE DAY OF THE LORD CAUSE YOU TO PERSEVERE IN YOUR PURSUIT OF CHRIST?

"Christ gives us faith, love, and His salvation."

WEEK 3 — day two

LIVING IN LIGHT OF THE END

READ 1 THESSALONIANS 5:1-11

In yesterday's reading, we studied the day of the Lord and how, on this day, God will bring justice to the wicked and peace to the righteous. We learned about this event by observing a few short verses that close the book of Malachi, but the day of the Lord is mentioned several times throughout the Old Testament and the New Testament (Isaiah 13:6, Jeremiah 46:10, Ezekiel 30:3, Acts 2:20). We can conclude that Scripture wants us to remember this day and treat it as significant.

But how do we do this? How do we remember the day of the Lord and let its coming motivate us to walk closely with God? Is this day supposed to terrify us or bring joy? These are all legitimate questions, and it is why we are going to pause in our reading of Malachi to read and discuss 1 Thessalonians, as Paul gives helpful answers to navigate this topic.

Paul and Silas began the church in Thessalonica. The people had responded strongly to the gospel, and many were converted to follow Christ. But when the Roman authorities learned of the rapidly growing church, they were concerned that their citizens would no longer honor Caesar as king, and wide persecution began. Paul writes 1 Thessalonians to the church to encourage and commend them because, despite their suffering, they held fast to the gospel.

At the conclusion of this letter, he speaks about the day of the Lord. The Thessalonians grieved the loss of loved ones who had died for their faith, and Paul reminds them of the hope of the resurrection. Those who have passed away will rise again, and the day of the Lord will gather together the family of God forever.

When Paul introduces the day of the Lord, he acknowledges that the believers are fully aware of this day. They do not know when it will come, but they know it is coming. And unlike those who rejected the Lord, believers will not be shocked or cower in shame when He does return. We will be full of joy. And we are to live in expectation of this day's arrival. We have been given the present day to exercise faithfulness to God, but because we do not know when the day of the Lord will be, we live as if that day could be today. When we remember that the Lord is returning, how we view our lives will begin to change. Some of the things that cause the most frustration today will not carry the same weight in eternity. It is not that a broken-down car or a toddler's tantrum are not important matters, but we will approach these situations differently in light of eternity. We must remember that everything we encounter today is preparing us for Christ's return.

Paul reminds the Thessalonians that peace and security are not found in this life. Any inkling of those things here will quickly fade away to remind us that this earth is not our forever home. The day of the Lord will bring the peace and security for which we long, but for others, the day will rip away any false idea they had of what peace and security look like. It will be taken from them, and only chaos and confusion will remain, for they do not know God. They are not prepared for what is coming. But because we have been prepared, we do know the end of the story, and we must tell them that true peace is found only in Jesus. He is the One who gives security for our souls, and when we know Him, we can give Him all of our fears.

Believers are no longer in the darkness of sin. We are in the light of the gospel, and we have Christ's light within us. We are not to dwell in darkness but in light, not becoming desensitized to the fact that the end is near. The day of the Lord gives us a proper perspective and should be sobering to us. As we face the darkness in anticipation of Christ's arrival, may we remember we have access to every spiritual blessing in Christ. Christ gives us faith, love, and His salvation.

We have been saved by our gracious and victorious Savior who will return and destroy all evil. We must not be afraid. May we instead encourage our brothers and sisters to persevere in their faith, knowing that this final day is coming, and it will surely come soon.

WE HAVE BEEN SAVED BY OUR GRACIOUS AND
VICTORIOUS SAVIOR WHO WILL RETURN
AND DESTROY ALL EVIL.

WHAT ARE SOME PRACTICAL WAYS YOU CAN TRAIN YOURSELF TO THINK OF THE DAY OF THE LORD? (CONSIDER A PHRASE OR PRAYER THAT YOU CAN REPEAT DAILY.)

———

HOW CAN YOU STAY AWAKE AND BE SELF-CONTROLLED IN YOUR DAY-TO-DAY LIFE LIKE PAUL DESCRIBES IN I THESSALONIANS 5:6?

———

HOW DOES THE GOSPEL TURN THE DAY OF THE LORD FROM SOMETHING FEARFUL TO A DAY OF JOY?

———

"Because of Jesus, the people of God finally become who they were always meant to become."

WEEK 3

REMEMBER HIS WORD

READ MALACHI 4:4-6

As we wrap up the book of Malachi and study these last verses that contain words from the Lord to His people, we must remember that the end of Malachi presents a dramatic pause between the Old Testament and the New Testament. Verses 4 to 6 of chapter 4 contains the final message the Lord wanted His people to hear before a long time of silence. The people already struggled to wait on the Lord, but now He was once more calling them to wait. Before the arrival of Christ and a period of waiting that would last hundreds of years, the Lord wanted His people to remember His Word.

In verse 4, the Lord tells Israel that they must remember the instruction He gave to Moses to give to them at Horeb. Horeb is an alternative name for Mount Sinai, the place where all of God's people gathered after He delivered them out of slavery in Egypt, saved them from Pharaoh's army, and parted the Red Sea so they could cross to safety. Mount Sinai was where Moses received the Law from the Lord—instruction that would show God's people how to keep their covenant with Him. Throughout the Old Testament, the people forgot this instruction, and they ran after other gods and idols. God continually disciplined and called them to repentance, and each time they repented, He restored them to Himself and asked them once again to remember His laws. The people's obedience to the Law would show their desire to keep their covenant with God. Following the Lord above their own desires would give them life and peace, even as they waited for the fulfillment of the Lord's promises.

As they kept the Law, they were not left in the dark. God tells them who they should look for in a Savior. The Lord says that "Elijah the prophet" is coming before the great and terrible day of judgment. He is the messenger of God who will prepare the people for God's final day of justice and salvation. But who is this messenger? Was he the literal prophet Elijah who was taken away in a flaming chariot by the Lord? We asked this question before at the beginning of chapter 3, when the Lord mentioned this messenger the first time. And the answer is the same. While John the Baptist is the first messenger the Lord sends—who walks in the footsteps of Elijah and calls the people to repentance—he is not the last messenger. The final messenger is Jesus, God in flesh. He is the last and greatest of all the prophets, and He is the last and greatest of all of God's priests. He is the greater Moses and the greater Elijah.

When we remember God's Word, we remember Christ, the fulfillment of all of its promises. He is our true deliverer, and He is the very Word of God. Jesus goes on our behalf before the Lord, just like Moses went on behalf of Israel. But Jesus, unlike Moses, fulfilled the covenant between God and His people. Moses helped initiate the old covenant between the Lord and Israel by presenting them with the Law God had given him. But Jesus began the new covenant between God and His people by fulfilling the Law through His atoning work on the cross and resurrection. The Law Moses gave meant spiritual death for the people because they could never have kept it. Jesus's sacrifice on our behalf meant that we could have life forever. He gave us salvation through trust in Him alone.

Just like Elijah, Jesus stands before the religious rulers of Israel and calls them to true worship of God. But Jesus is not only calling them away from idolatry and false teaching; Jesus is calling them to Himself because He is God. Jesus reveals that He is the way, the truth, and the life. And while Elijah prophesied about the coming of the rain and miracles performed, Jesus, the Creator of the world in the flesh, shows His authority over all of creation. He calms the storms, and He brings the dead back to life. Then He provides eternal life for all who believe in Him. All of the Law and all of the prophets point to Christ.

The book of Malachi ends by telling us what the messenger, Christ, will do. He will turn the hearts of fathers back to their sons, and he will turn the hearts of sons back to their fathers. He brings reconciliation between God and us, but He also brings reconciliation within the family of God. We are restored to our heavenly Father in Christ, but we are also restored to our spiritual family. Our peace with God means we are finally at peace with others. Because of Jesus, the people of God finally become who they were always meant to become.

The Lord warns the people once more that if they do not turn to obedience, even after the arrival of the messenger, He will strike the land with a curse. Rejecting Christ does not lead to life. It leads to life under the effects of sin.

The messenger who Malachi foretold did come, and He brought life, peace, and reconciliation. We now await His arrival again, and we are sober-minded as we remember His Word. The day when Jesus returns will fill our hearts with joy because we have been restored to God. We are God's children, and we belong to Him. But for those who reject God, the appearance of Christ will bring about eternal death, a sobering consequence. As we remember Christ's Word, we must speak it to others so that they can know Christ. We must go forward with His message as we wait. We must make war on the curse that lays heavy on mankind, and we rejoice that we have been given all things in our Savior.

We are God's children, and we belong to Him

IF GOD'S FINAL MESSAGE TO HIS PEOPLE BEFORE A PERIOD OF SILENCE WAS TO REMEMBER HIS WORD, HOW DO YOU THINK BELIEVERS SHOULD TREAT SCRIPTURE AS WE WAIT ON CHRIST'S RETURN?

———

READ LUKE 9:28-36. WHO ARE THE TWO PEOPLE JESUS TALKS TO DURING HIS TRANSFIGURATION? WHY IS THIS IMPORTANT, AND WHAT DOES IT SYMBOLIZE? (HINT: HOW DO THESE PEOPLE POINT TO CHRIST?)

———

WHAT ARE TWO WAYS YOU CAN BEGIN TO SHARE THE GOSPEL WITH SOMEONE IN YOUR COMMUNITY THIS WEEK? WHY SHOULD YOU BE MOTIVATED TO SHARE?

———

"Jesus, the final messenger, initiated the arrival of this kingdom as He proclaimed the gospel."

WEEK 3

AFTER THE OLD TESTAMENT

READ DANIEL 2

After we finish the last few words of the book of Malachi, we flip the page and discover a blank space. Our Bibles usually have one or two pages between the Old Testament and New Testament to signal a break in time. But what we do not see from this blank page is 400 years of history that transpires before Jesus arrives on earth and when God speaks once more.

After Israel receives the Lord's message from the prophet Malachi, the world is set ablaze with tumultuous changes as empires rise and fall. What is incredible is that all of these changes were predicted by the prophet Daniel. When Judah fell into the hands of the Babylonians, many of their young men were brought into the court of the King of Babylon, Nebuchadnezzar. Some were able to advance and achieve status in this new world, and Daniel was one of them. But Nebuchadnezzar was a testy king, and when he had a dream that frightened him, he gave his wise men an impossible task. They would need to tell him the dream and interpret it, and if no wise man could do so, they and their families would be killed. But Daniel asked the king if he could give him more time, and he and his friends prayed that God would grant him a revelation. And the Lord did.

What Daniel saw in his dream was the exact history that occurred throughout the last books of the Bible and the time represented in the break between the Old Testament and New Testament. Nebuchadnezzar's dream revealed a statue with four parts consisting of different metals. Each metal piece was another kingdom that would tear down the one before. The head of the statue was gold, and it represented Babylon and King Nebuchadnezzar. The chest and arms of the statue were silver, and they represented the next empire—that of the Medo-Persians. They would conquer Babylon, and eventually, they would allow God's people to return home and build their land, walls, and temple. The stomach and thighs of the statue were bronze, and Daniel told Nebuchadnezzar that this kingdom would rule the entire earth. This was the Greek empire that quickly conquered the world because of the advancement of Alexander the Great. And lastly, the statue had legs of iron, representing the Roman empire, because they would smash every other empire in their path. But a stone came and struck the whole statue and turned it to chaff, and this stone grew into a mountain that filled the whole earth.

The mountain was the final and unshakable kingdom of God that the first messenger, John the Baptist, proclaimed was at hand. Jesus, the final messenger, initiated the arrival of this kingdom as He proclaimed the gospel. This is the kingdom that Jesus rules and we are a part of today, but someday this kingdom will physically come to earth and destroy all sin and evil. And we will live in this kingdom forever.

So as the people of God waited and waited for new revelation from the Lord, it was not as though there was nothing happening around them. The world was changing. Even the culture of the Old Testament to the New Testament dramatically shifted. But God's people were always spared, and they persisted, even despite terrible persecution and suffering. Remember what the Lord told them in Malachi 3:6: "Because I, the Lord, have not changed, you descendants of Jacob have not been destroyed." They would never cease to be His, and though God did not give them new words in these 400 years before Christ's arrival, He was preserving them and preparing them for His coming. Though they did not have a new word of revelation, they had God's Word that was previously recorded. They could hold onto His promises amid their distress.

In the New Testament, when Christ is born, the world is very different from what it had been in Malachi. In Malachi, Israel was under the control of the Medo-Persian empire. When Christ is born, the Romans are ruling. The Persians were much more friendly to the Jews than the Romans. The Pharisees and Sadducees, two groups of leading religious Jews, were very influential in Israel. These groups were not well established in the book of Malachi, but when the book of Matthew opens, they are some of the most important leaders in Jewish society. Greek has become the language of the day in Jesus's time because of the world-dominating empire of Alexander the Great. The Hebrew Scriptures have actually been translated into Greek in a work called the Septuagint. What is amazing about the Greek language being so widespread is that it significantly aided the advancement of the gospel because most people across the world were familiar with the Greek language.

God may not have been actively speaking through His prophets to His people during the 400 years of silence, but He was actively working. God was moving all the pieces of history and setting the scene for the fullness of time—the time when His Son would be born. So as we wait today for His return, hoping and longing to see His face, we can remember that just like God was orchestrating all the pieces of His plan and using the empires of the world to do so, He is doing the same today. God is working behind the scenes, and His sovereign hand can comfort us. When the time comes for Jesus's second arrival, we will finally be able to live physically in His kingdom. The new kingdom will be an unshakable one that causes all other kingdoms, empires, and rulers to crumble. Jesus is coming soon, and in this, we have great joy!

GOD IS WORKING BEHIND THE SCENES, AND His sovereign hand can comfort us.

WHAT DO YOU LEARN ABOUT THE LORD BY SEEING HOW DANIEL'S INTERPRETATION OF NEBUCHADNEZZAR'S DREAM WAS FULFILLED IN THE HISTORY OF THE WORLD?

———

WHY IS IT IMPORTANT TO KNOW THE HISTORY OF WHAT HAPPENED BETWEEN THE OLD AND NEW TESTAMENTS?

———

READ PSALM 27:14 AND PSALM 37:34. HOW DO YOU PROPERLY WAIT FOR THE LORD TO ACT?

———

NEBUCHADNEZZAR'S DREAM

Nebuchadnezzar's dream revealed a statue with four parts consisting of different metals. Each metal piece was another kingdom that would tear down the one before.

HEAD OF GOLD
The head represented Babylon and King Nebuchadnezzar.

CHEST AND ARMS OF SILVER
They represented the next empire—that of the Medo-Persians. They would conquer Babylon, and eventually, they would allow God's people to return home and build their land, walls, and temple.

STOMACH AND THIGHS OF BRONZE
Daniel told Nebuchadnezzar that this kingdom would rule the entire earth. This was the Greek empire that quickly conquered the world because of the advancement of Alexander the Great.

LEGS OF IRON
This represented the Roman empire, because they would smash every other empire in their path.

"May Christ's presence in the book of Malachi fill your heart with great longing and anticipation for the day of His second coming!"

THE GOSPEL IN MALACHI

READ "WHAT IS THE GOSPEL?" ON PAGE 88,
GENESIS 3, ROMANS 3:23, ROMANS 6:23, 2 CORINTHIANS 5:21

As we read our Bibles and dig into the glories of God's Word, we must always come back to whom Scripture consistently points us: Jesus. When we study Scripture without Him in mind, we miss the big picture of what God is trying to do in His story of redemption. The Old Testament introduces us to Christ at the very beginning of God's story, after Adam and Eve sinned and rejected God. He is the promised offspring in Genesis 3:15 who will restore humanity to the Lord. The Israelites' struggles represent humanity's need for the Lord as they wander from the Lord and disobey His commands. While they have many great earthly leaders who seem as though they could be the Messiah, all of them fall short. Abraham, Moses, and David were all revered men in Israel's history who loved the Lord, but they were not perfect. They could not save Israel from their sins. Only Jesus could do that because He never sinned. He was the only One who could become a perfect sacrifice for the sins of God's people. He was the only One who could atone for sin forever. The book of Malachi shows the people's need for Christ once more and foreshadows His arrival.

As you wrap up this study, it is beneficial to re-read the book of Malachi and remind yourself of how the Lord has revealed Christ throughout its pages. The following questions are included to guide you through each chapter. This may be a day of the study that you allow yourself more time. Consider spending today and tomorrow reading Malachi and completing these questions. May Christ's presence in the book of Malachi fill your heart with great longing and anticipation for the day of His second coming!

CHAPTER 1

What specific verses remind you of Christ in chapter 1 of Malachi?

How does Christ's obedience contrast the disobedience or sin of those mentioned in the passage? (e.g., the priests of Israel treat God's altar with contempt—how do Jesus's actions contrast theirs?)

How does Christ fulfill the promises given within the passage?

CHAPTER 2

What specific verses remind you of Christ in chapter 2 of Malachi?

How does Christ's obedience contrast the disobedience or sin of those mentioned in the passage?

How does Christ fulfill the promises given within the passage?

CHAPTER 3

What specific verses remind you of Christ in chapter 3 of Malachi?

How does Christ's obedience contrast the disobedience and sin of those mentioned in the passage?

How does Christ fulfill the promises given within the passage?

CHAPTER 4

What specific verses remind you of Christ in chapter 4 of Malachi?

How does Christ's obedience contrast the disobedience and sin of those mentioned in the passage?

How does Christ fulfill the promises given within the passage?

How has what you have learned about Christ in the book of Malachi deepened your understanding of the gospel?

How do these truths about Christ change how you should live?

week three Scripture memory

MALACHI 4:2

BUT FOR YOU WHO FEAR MY NAME,
THE SUN OF RIGHTEOUSNESS WILL RISE
WITH HEALING IN ITS WINGS, AND YOU WILL
GO OUT AND PLAYFULLY JUMP LIKE
CALVES FROM THE STALL.

week three reflection

PARAPHRASE A SECTION FROM THIS WEEK'S PASSAGES THAT STOOD OUT TO YOU THE MOST.

WHAT DID YOU OBSERVE FROM THIS WEEK'S TEXT ABOUT GOD AND HIS CHARACTER?

WHAT DO THESE PASSAGES TEACH YOU ABOUT THE CONDITION OF MANKIND AND YOURSELF?

REVIEW MALACHI 4:1-6, I THESSALONIANS 5:1-11, AND DANIEL 2

HOW DO THESE PASSAGES POINT TO THE GOSPEL?

IN LIGHT OF WHAT YOU HAVE READ, HOW SHOULD YOU RESPOND TO THESE PASSAGES?

WHAT ARE TWO ACTION STEPS YOU CAN TAKE THIS WEEK TO APPLY THESE PASSAGES TO YOUR LIFE?

Weekly Reflection

What is the Gospel?

THANK YOU FOR READING AND ENJOYING THIS STUDY WITH US! WE ARE ABUNDANTLY GRATEFUL FOR THE WORD OF GOD, THE INSTRUCTION WE GLEAN FROM IT, AND THE EVER-GROWING UNDERSTANDING IT PROVIDES FOR US OF GOD'S CHARACTER. WE ARE ALSO THANKFUL THAT SCRIPTURE CONTINUALLY POINTS TO ONE THING IN INNUMERABLE WAYS: THE GOSPEL.

We remember our brokenness when we read about the fall of Adam and Eve in the garden of Eden (Genesis 3), where sin entered into a perfect world and maimed it. We remember the necessity that something innocent must die to pay for our sin when we read about the atoning sacrifices in the Old Testament. We read that we have all sinned and fallen short of the glory of God (Romans 3:23) and that the penalty for our brokenness, the wages of our sin, is death (Romans 6:23). We all need grace and mercy, but most importantly, we all need a Savior.

We consider the goodness of God when we realize that He did not plan to leave us in this dire state. We see His promise to buy us back from the clutches of sin and death in Genesis 3:15. And we see that promise accomplished with Jesus Christ on the cross. Jesus Christ knew no sin yet became sin so that we might become righteous through His sacrifice (2 Corinthians 5:21). Jesus was tempted in every way that we are and lived sinlessly. He was reviled yet still yielded Himself for our sake, that we may have life abundant in Him. Jesus lived the perfect life that we could not live and died the death that we deserved.

The gospel is profound yet simple. There are many mysteries in it that we will never understand this side of heaven, but there is still overwhelming weight to its implications in this life. The gospel tells of our sinfulness and God's goodness and a gracious gift that compels a response. We are saved by grace through faith, which means that we rest with faith in the grace that Jesus Christ displayed on the cross (Ephesians 2:8-9). We cannot save ourselves from our brokenness or do any amount of good works to merit God's favor. Still, we can have faith that what Jesus accomplished in His death, burial, and resurrection was more than enough for our salvation and our eternal delight. When we accept God, we are commanded to die to ourselves and our sinful desires and live a life worthy of the calling we have received (Ephesians 4:1). The gospel compels us to be sanctified, and in so doing, we are conformed to the likeness of Christ Himself. This is hope. This is redemption. This is the gospel.

SCRIPTURES TO REFERENCE:

GENESIS 3:15	*I will put hostility between you and the woman, and between your offspring and her offspring. He will strike your head, and you will strike his heel.*
ROMANS 3:23	*For all have sinned and fall short of the glory of God.*
ROMANS 6:23	*For the wages of sin is death, but the gift of God is eternal life in Christ Jesus our Lord.*
2 CORINTHIANS 5:21	*He made the one who did not know sin to be sin for us, so that in him we might become the righteousness of God.*
EPHESIANS 2:8-9	*For you are saved by grace through faith, and this is not from yourselves; it is God's gift—not from works, so that no one can boast.*
EPHESIANS 4:1-3	*Therefore I, the prisoner in the Lord, urge you to walk worthy of the calling you have received, with all humility and gentleness, with patience, bearing with one another in love, making every effort to keep the unity of the Spirit through the bond of peace.*

The messenger who Malachi foretold did come, and He brought life, peace, and reconciliation.

—

We now await His arrival again, and we are sober-minded as we remember His Word.

Thank you for studying God's Word with us

CONNECT WITH US
@thedailygraceco
@dailygracepodcast

CONTACT US
info@thedailygraceco.com

SHARE
#thedailygraceco

VISIT US ONLINE
www.thedailygraceco.com

MORE DAILY GRACE
The Daily Grace App
Daily Grace Podcast